KNOWLEDGE IS POWER BUT

ACCESS IS DIVINE

We Must Be Granted **Access** to Obtain Knowledge

Knowledge Is Power but **Access** Is Divine

We Must Be Granted **Access** to Obtain Knowledge

by
Melvin E. Alleman

DORRANCE PUBLISHING CO

EST. 1920

PITTSBURGH, PENNSYLVANIA 15238

Dorrance Publishing Co
585 Alpha Drive
Pittsburgh, PA 15238
Visit our website at www.dorrancebookstore.com

ISBN: 979-8-89127-624-6
eISBN: 979-8-89127-122-7

Preface

You often hear the statement; "knowledge is power". This is likely based on a belief that somehow, we all became or are expecting to become more valuable because we learned valuable skills (and potentially cheats and/or hacks) along life's journey.

Knowledge could indeed get you promoted at work to a position of power (leadership, supervisory), and often there are "friends/family members" that will only associate with you to benefit from your knowledge, which gives you power over them. But how is knowledge obtained? I am suggesting here that knowledge is obtained via **access**. **Access** is the ultimate power.

Access, I believe, often comes from divine intervention. Divine, as I am purposefully defining it here is, "of or from God". Where you see **access** in bold print, it is where I believe the power of God was involved at these points in my life.

Divine intervention in one's life does not have to be dramatic events that deliver one from some tragedy or health condition into complete protection or healing. It does not have to be the result of intense prayer. It can be any interference of deity in one's life, perhaps an answer to a prayer we didn't even request because we didn't even know to ask for it.

This story is my attempt at age fifty-nine to recount numerous times that God has intervened in my life to grant me **access** to pathways and gates, which ultimately allowed me to arrive where I am in life today.

If you are looking for a lot of negativities here, you will not find it. All of the interesting stuff that can be held against me some day has been omitted.

Chapter 1

The Early Years

My story starts in the year 1963. I was born the third child in the John H. Alleman family. We resided at Star Route 3, Box 56, in a part of rural Pennsylvania known as Lurgan Township. Rolling hills and farms everywhere. My mom was forty-four and my dad was fifty-two years old when I was born. Not a typical family structure per se, but anyone raised by their grandparents would understand the dynamics of this atypical age difference between parent and child.

My oldest brother Jaye was twenty-four years older than I. He had already been in the PA National Guard, moved to Shippensburg, was married, and had one child (my nephew Kevin), all before I was even born. Imagine having to call someone younger than you "Uncle Melvin". Kevin did that.

Dennis was the next brother, about four and a half years older.

The house that I grew up in was built by my dad on a half-acre piece of land carved out of a ten-acre plot of land owned by my paternal grandparents. I never knew my paternal grandfather Ira; he died the same year I was born.

A have heard a lot of people who work normal jobs telling their co-worker, "I am building a new house up on Horse Valley Road." Most of them are just having it built for them, not within their capability to actually build it themselves.

I did know my paternal grandmother Bertha. She lived in Lurgan in a little mobile home (which is still there vacant today). After Ira died, they sold the house where my dad, uncles, and aunt grew up. Jaye had experienced going across the yard next door to grandma's house, but I would not.

I never knew my maternal grandfather Albert, he died when my mother was only ten years old. He was a WWI veteran that was wounded in combat. I did know my maternal grandmother Sarah and her new husband "Chub" Henry. They lived in Scotland, PA.

I was blessed with a family that may not have shown evidence of a strong relationship with God, but they did not drink alcohol, or abuse us or anyone else. I indeed lived a "sheltered life", as some would call it. If they had truly been disciples of God, it would have been more evident in their lives.

My oldest brother Jaye actually taught Sunday school and led Bible studies, even did so over the radio airwaves on WSHP 1480AM, Shippensburg PA.

I had **access** to Mongul church every Sunday, which gave me knowledge of God and his teachings. I once heard someone say that all children are born to know the difference between right and wrong. This may be true but without the right parents or **access** to godly folks at church, you can quickly have that knowledge overwritten by a lot of bad. If you do not know God, that is either by your own choices or you may not have been given **access** to friends/family with a godly lifestyle.

I chose to be saved from my sins at the age of thirteen, "sprinkling" was my choice of baptism. The thought of being dunked in the Conodoquinet creek down the hill from the church scared me.

I had **access** to Lurgan Elementary School, Chambersburg Area Middle School, Faust Junior High School, and Chambersburg Area Senior High School (99.9% attendance). If you as a reader went to a better school than I, it was because God gave you **access** to it, either by buying your way in or by the geographic location that you would be destined to live.

We would often visit family, although I would never really establish any relevant relationships from these visits. I just did not comprehend how to make friends, I suppose; I was NOT blessed with that ability. I remember being bullied more than befriended at school and on the bus; I am not sure why.

I did not have any pets of my own either, although an outdoor cat that came around could have come close. I didn't establish relationships well with pets or people. I have heard people often tell others not to trust someone who doesn't love pets, I guess I am not to be trusted then.

Most of my time was spent watching our vacuum tube amplified black/white television set. I did not go outside much, definitely did not associate much with neighbors, and made very few friends at school.

I had **access** to books, therefore the knowledge in them, but just wasn't interested in reading them. The action of turning words into thoughts appears to consume a lot of my brain's processing power. After reading 100 pages, I sometimes can't remember key details about the story. I would have to read it several times to grasp it all. Even today, I can watch an entire movie without learning all of the relevant character's names.

My dad was gone a lot, working on the maintenance crew at the Shippensburg State Teachers College (now known as Shippensburg University) by day, and on whatever house in Lurgan Township needed construction or remodeling by night and on Saturday. He never worked on Sunday, but if there were no family reunions on schedule, he went to his friend Jack Herr's house to visit in the afternoon. If it was too rainy to work on houses, he went to the local hangout Stouffer's Garage to visit. The garage had a row of chairs there where "old geezers" would go to hang out even if their car wasn't in the shop.

Dad was a charter member of the Lurgan Township Lions Club and was heavily involved in the construction of the buildings and pavilions there. From this, I learned something about being a part of a service-oriented organization.

Access to my dad's companionship was limited to following him around occasionally as he worked or visited. I don't remember getting too much knowledge from following him around, but I undoubtedly picked something up along the way. After all, I do my own construction and remodeling at my house. Being self-sufficient has saved me a lot of cash over the years.

He would sleep every Sunday in church. My joke is that my dad only had three modes of operation, working, eating, and sleeping. He was heavily involved in the construction of the building and its renovations.

Saturday evenings were the only time we actually spent as a family. There were auctions (my dad liked these for some reason), and local fairs and festivals (I liked these).

My mom was home almost all the time, therefore so was I. She didn't work and didn't have a driver's license. She paid Aunt Minerva or others to take us to the bank and stores. We were never gone for more than a couple of hours.

These trips gave me **access** to a bank in Orrstown. Yes, Orrstown Bank started in Orrstown, PA, not Shippensburg. It was not a branch to be closed like the employees of the bank believe today. It was THE only bank building during the period 1919 until 1981. I also had **access** to Cressler's Fruit Market (where Turkey Hill convenience store is today), and other stores.

I don't have supporting documentation of this, but I believe my mother would today appear somewhere on the "autistic spectrum" mentally. There is a popular movie about a severely autistic gentleman known as Raymond, but she was not like that. I call her "highly functioning" in layman's terms. She always did laundry on Monday, always went to the grocery store on Wednesday. If Minerva couldn't take her by day, then Dad would have to take her that same evening. All of the newspapers had to be stacked in chronological order.

If they were knocked down for some reason, it was traumatic for her and it had to be reworked at once. We always had hamburgers/hot dogs cooked in the same skillet for Sunday lunch if there were no family reunions on the schedule. She only washed the car on Saturday.

She hoarded everything including paper napkins from restaurants and birthday cards/gifts from givers. The hoarding DEFINITELY altered my life story. The clutter and dust were everywhere, there were whole rooms that were off limits. The dining room and kitchen table were off limits, so we dined on the enclosed "back porch". One of only two bedrooms was off limits, so my brother slept on the living room couch, and I slept in the bathroom on a cot.

Yes, we did this for many years, not just as a temporary solution to a construction project. This was the limited **access** that God provided me in early life. I never invited anyone to my house growing up, and I continue to be stressed and disgusted by hoarding.

It is conceivable that my siblings, my children, and my grandchildren all appear somewhere on the autism spectrum as well. It is my joke at home that I am 50%, my kids are 25%, and my grandchildren are 12%, but obviously autism is much more complicated than that.

I am pretty sure that my brother Jaye appeared somewhere on the autistic spectrum as well. It was stated by his son Curt during his funeral that he always had the same schedule during his vacations to the beach. Always left the house at 6 AM, stopped at the same restaurant in Lancaster for breakfast, arrived at the same hotel at 11 AM, and so on.

My knowledge would not have expanded very much if I had stayed on this path, but soon there would be more.

In fourth grade at school, our class was given a hearing test that involved listening to tones and answering questions about the tones. The way I remember this story, only two of us in the class passed the test because we were the only students offered to play stringed instruments.

My parents supported me by renting a violin. Finally, **access** to something constructive to do with my time. I played it at home all the time and even at church occasionally. I had more than the normal amount of time to practice than other kids with more normal social experience, so I became quite good. This was God providing me **access** to an increased level of self-esteem.

Some people who knew me as a youngster would say that I didn't really need an increase in self-esteem, they would say that I thoroughly enjoyed "showing off" as evidenced by my loud singing during elementary school musical performances. I was told that I often "drowned out" the others in my class numerous times over the years.

I was a very fast learner, so I was quickly pulled ahead of my peers in ability, which built confidence. Over time I would learn that I was gifted with the ability to achieve steep learning curves on almost everything I attempted (as long as it could be done with only minimal reading), but then I would get satisfied with my ability and stop pushing myself to achieve excellence.

At the coaxing of my teacher, my parents invested in a custom-made violin from the Chimney's Violin shop in Boiling Springs, PA. They supported me with private lessons at Wilson college and encouraged me to participate in the symphony orchestra, but I had to figure out how to get to the lessons with Dad working a lot and Mom not driving. A friend at school, Warren allowed me to get off the bus at his house, which was within walking distance. The Guyer, Gill, and Swanger families had children in the orchestra as well, so they would alternate picking me up from our house.

Chapter 2

Freedom

At age thirteen, my mother had to go to the hospital due to low circulation in her legs resulting in leaking ulcers. I stayed at my Aunt Dorothy's for a couple of weeks. This would be my first "sleepover" in a place other than my home. She babysat a neighbor who lived near them, so I would have some daytime interaction with another child, but I don't remember his name. It was there that I had my first **access** to a bicycle. He taught me to ride it, so then I wanted one of my own!

I was age fourteen when my dad turned sixty-five years old. Even though he was still working, we started receiving three Social Security checks in the mail, one for Mom, one for my brother Dennis, and one for me. The way I remember the story, the government was contacted to ascertain the validity of these checks, since Dad was not retired yet. The end result was us cashing them and continually receiving them, mine until I reached the age of eighteen and my brother until he completed college.

I once told this story to a civics teacher at my high school during a class session covering government programs, but he didn't believe it. So, from that perspective I guess having unsolicited checks arriving in your mailbox for years could have been divine intervention...perhaps.

I opened a checking account at Orrstown Bank, as amazingly enough Mom allowed Dennis and I to keep the money received in our names. I believe this was God providing me the **access** the funds required to change my life story!

So, now how to get that bicycle?

Well, as I stated we went to the grocery store every Wednesday. Across the street was a Western Auto store that sold bicycles. In May 1977, I made a deal to buy one. The man at the counter stated that he knew where I lived (was friends with Dad) and offered to deliver it to me. It arrived after 5 PM closing that evening. I was free!

I started riding it wherever and whenever I wanted. Mom and Dad had lost control at that point. The "helicopter" style of parenting was over. I rode over 4,300 miles the first year. I still honored the critical parent directed points on schedule, school, and church, so I wasn't totally off the rails. But now, I was now accessing everything I could within a reasonable distance. I started riding at first just to get away, riding to Shippensburg to stores and food. It was easier to get to town than it was to get home, mostly because the prevailing wind would be in my face heading west on Roxbury Rd, but partially because we lived on nearly the highest elevation around.

There was Henry's store in Mongul that had a bench outside I could take a break at on the way home. Getting to Roxbury was easier, there was George's Market that also had a bench outside for break time. I often thought of climbing Forge Hill, but the thought of my brakes failing coming back down scared me.

I would ride to Sunrise Electronics and Radio Shack in Chambersburg. **Access** to these stores allowed me to see what was actually available in the form of electronic components.

I used my continued **access** to funds and stores to add accessories to my bike. It started with lights and a rechargeable battery pack, but it progressed to way beyond reasonable and customary. I had a Citizens Band radio connected to a whip antenna designed for a car, and a cassette player connected to speakers on the handlebars. Ultimately, I rode over 4,200 miles the first year.

Later, I joined the Pleasant Hall Fire Department (PHFD) as a junior member, and that provided me with a sense of duty and a more purposeful destination. I rode on the back step of the fire engines on calls, a practice that is no longer allowed today.

I rode my bike to training, fundraising efforts, meetings, and even some fire calls. even a funky siren set-up that is still remembered today by the current fire chief of PHFD (he was a kid then living on Lurgan Road). Erector set pieces were my materials of choice, I simply did not have the knowledge (or **access**) to other materials.

There, however, was some negative **access** from being around firefighters that was clearly not divine, **access** to alcohol, specifically beer. Almost everyone in the fire department were drinkers. I, however, was gifted with the ability to recognize that alcohol was not for me. The ability to know right from wrong is a gift from God! My first beer ended up poured down behind the back seat of a car on the ride home from fire training one year. I won't get in trouble for saying this now, the owner of the car passed away years ago in a tractor roll-over accident.

The second year of bike riding started with a new bike with "disk brakes", cutting edge at the time. I put another 3,800 miles on that one.

I even became the youngest Emergency Medical Technician in the state of Pennsylvania. I say the youngest because I lied about my age and completed the course at age fifteen. You had to be sixteen to be certified at the time. That would later catch up with me when two years later I was asked by the ambulance chief if I wanted to drive an ambulance. I knew it was time to self-report then.

I recently learned watching a Sunday evening news program reporting that medical studies show that heroes instinctively respond to emergency situations due to a section of their brain reacting to thoughts of persons or animals being in distress. I didn't really feel that; I was just there for something relevant to do. I learned from that experience that the medical field was difficult and was not something that I wanted to do long term.

I remember doing CPR twice during my rides in the ambulance. The first time was a robbery suspect at the 7-Eleven in Greenvillage. He attempted to flee across US-11 and was hit by a car. With a gash in the back of his head it seemed futile, but we were required to perform CPR all the way to the hospital until someone with the proper authority can pronounce someone dead.

The second time was a train wreck in Pinola, we did CPR on him as well to the hospital.

We once found a person in Roxbury that had been dead for days in Roxbury, after responding to a non-emergency wellness check. We found him sitting in his chair in the living room. We stuffed Vicks VapoRub up our noses and hauled him to a funeral home in Shippensburg.

I never really entered a burning building to search for or save anyone, junior members were not authorized to do that. I once went to another fire station in a suburb of Baltimore to experience what frequent fire calls were like, but I slept through them all anyway. I was a really hard sleeper.

I found my first real girlfriend from hanging out at the fire department, Christine who lived in Pleasant Hall. Received my first kiss in the dark alley beside the old fire hall. We could not date publicly though; her father Wayne would not allow that to happen until she was age sixteen.

Then I was able to obtain a car, a 1967 Plymouth Fury III leftover from my brother. He bought a new 1977 Plymouth Volare when I was age fifteen so the Fury sat in the yard for a long time, all I could do with it at the time was add a sound system and sit in it as a getaway during weather not suitable for bike riding.

I did take it for a drive once before I officially "learned" to drive. I only almost wrecked once on a sharp curve on Lurgan road. A Fury is a big car without good handling ability, but I guess I learned about physics on that day. Later in drivers' education class, I learned that as speed doubles, forces square.

When I obtained a driver's license at age sixteen, the bike riding abruptly stopped. Its purpose was transportation, not exercise or pleasure, so it stayed parked on the front porch until a co-worker Earl bought it. It was expendable, it served its purpose by providing the **access** I needed when I needed it.

Of course, the adding of accessories continued with the car, there was always something being added to it or reworked on it.

Eventually I bought a second 1967 Fury, this one was a "Sport Fury", with a 383 cubic inch engine. I never did like it though; it didn't accelerate as well even though it had a bigger engine.

Chapter 3

Companionship

One day at the start of a new school year at age fourteen, I boarded the bus to school and was invited to sit next to Rob who was just starting middle school that year. We got to talking about bike riding and he thought we could perhaps ride bikes together sometime. He invited me to his house on Mongul Road, and I accepted.

I only ever remember being invited to someone's house once before, for a birthday party for Carla. It could have been one of those requirements from her parents to invite everyone from the class since we never really were friends.

I often went to Ginger's house, a preschool friend, but I didn't count that as an invite because our fathers were fellow Lions Club members and Dad and I often ended up at her house. But I did consider Ginger to be my "girlfriend" during my elementary school years.

I remember Rob's mother Janet being very gracious and hospitable, so I genuinely felt welcome there. Later I would learn the Leidigs had **access** to God, attending church in Newburg.

For months on end, I remember just showing up at the house and Rob and I going off on bike rides together. Rob was allowed to go as long as the daily farm chores were done.

One year, we even picked up litter at the Shippensburg Fairgrounds during fair week each day, which took us to town more than once per day that week. When Frank was president of the fair commission, trash was picked up through a process where interested workers would show up each day at 7 AM and we would be picked as employees based on the order we arrived. The only problem with that was we would not be paid until the fair was over.

We figured out Faygo Red Pop was the best drink at warm temperatures. It was impossible to keep fluids cold on long bike rides on hot days. We are both lucky to be alive today, it is very dangerous riding on the same roads as cars and trucks. Frequency and duration were both high, however there were no cell phones and GPS to distract drivers as there are today.

Eventually our bike rides became less frequent, as I became active in the PHFD, and he became active as the drummer for the Cornerstone Quartet gospel group, but I continued to visit him.

One visit to Rob's house when his cousins were there, the Nearons family. The Leidigs would be frequented by family visitors such as the Nearons, and less often the Berts and the Fernbaughs, who lived further away. It was there that I met Crystal, who ultimately became my spouse. So, I figured my **access** to my future family started with an invitation from a fellow bus rider.

The bond between Crystal and I grew stronger when I attended the Valley Barn dance in Spring Run. The Valley Dance was a long building in Spring Run, owned by Vince Gettel and the Bluegrass Cut-ups would have square dancing every Saturday night. The Nearons and the Leidigs would all go there, so I did as well.

At one point, I would try to change (or screw up) my destiny by inviting my old girlfriend Christine to a dance at the local Lions Club building, but we eventually got past that.

I believe there was divine intervention in my marriage to Crystal. My Vo-tech teacher once asked me, "How did you get a girl like her?" I don't remember my response, but I guess the comment meant that I was not a likely candidate for marriage.

In the state of Pennsylvania at the time we were married, parental permission was needed since she was seventeen years old. That **access** was granted as well as her mother provided the necessary consent. I am sure God spoke to her at some point in the process, but she probably regretted it later. There wasn't much else that Priscilla and I agreed on.

Today, you can't marry at age seventeen in Pennsylvania even with parental permission.

I would go on to have another close friend during high school, Donald (Donny), whom I met at Vo-tech. Rob and Donny would both participate in my wedding as best man and usher.

Before I got married, I got rid of all of the jacked up, rigged up "Fury" stuff, and bought newer and more reliable transportation.

Chapter 4

A Future Career

One of the items that Mom bought me as a child at Nichols department store (where Hobby Lobby is now in Chambersburg) was a "Logix Kosmos Super Electronics 1" set (which I still have). This kit was a personal choice that facilitated the development of potential career choice in electronics technology. At some point in middle school all students were required to talk to the guidance counselor about career choices, but I believe I had already developed an interest in electronics technology.

My dad had a friend Jake, who had a son named Sid, who was several years older than me. Sid was working at Letterkenny Army Depot during his senior year as a co-op student. I didn't know at the time what co-op meant; I only saw that he was driving a new car as a high school student. I wanted a job like that someday, after all my social security checks would end at age eighteen if I didn't pursue college.

My guidance counselor at Middle School advised that most of the graduates of the Franklin County Vocational-Technical school get to do that. The counselor advised that if I passed "Algebra I" in ninth grade and applied for **access** to the Electronics Technology course, I would likely be able to do that as well. This required a passing grade in Algebra I in grade 9, so that is the learning path I completed.

I knew about Letterkenny as I passed it every day on the school bus and had toured the depot many times on Armed Forces Day open house events.

The learning path worked! Early in twelfth grade, five of us were directed to leave school in the middle of the day for an interview in Building 500. No application required. All five of us were hired and we started in Oct. 1980 as Electronics Workers Wage Grade 1. **Access** granted!

Eventually those of us that truly wanted to make the depot our employment future were hired as full-time career conditional employees as Wage Grade 5 after our high school graduation. Try doing that today! Only Donny Grove and I stuck around more than the first 5 years, the other three moved on to other things.

Now, just to recap, I possess the following gifts basically handed to me at this point through divine intervention:

1. **Access** to transportation
2. **Access** to steady employment
3. **Access** to my future family unit.

Yes, I had to pass the courses. Yes, I had to answer the questions in the interview successfully. But the knowledge required to achieve these was provided by the **access** granted to me at each checkpoint. I didn't earn these!

Chapter 5

Housekeeping

1981-1991

I am now at the point in this story where life events are happening concurrently, job and family. I would graduate high school in June, be married by October, and have my first child Anthony in April. I would eventually have three children, Anthony, Daryl, and Ashley.

My mother used to call getting married and starting a family, "housekeeping". That is what she said Dad and her did in Mongul back in 1939. For Crystal and me, this started in 1982.

We shopped for and purchased our first mobile home to be placed in the Shippensburg Mobile Estates, although it was Crystal's grandfather Aaron that facilitated us getting a vacant lot there. At the time it was the premier trailer park in town, with many on the waiting list.

Like I stated before, all five of us "Vo-Techers" in the class of 1981 (as we called by other workers at the depot) were hired and started on the same day. They all started in Building #370, but for some reason I started in Building #51. They would all tell stories about how fun their jobs were sitting at a workbench in an environmentally controlled atmosphere, but I was disassembling dirty old HAWK missile system Platoon Command Post (PCP) shelters coming in for rebuild in a cold 1940s style warehouse building. Nothing was fun about that.

I am intentionally spelling HAWK as all capital letters, because originally the original equipment manufacturer would break the system name out as an acronym, Homing All the Way Killer.

I did manage to get kicked out of the position though. I was working with and being mentored by Lacey, who had a process for taking an entire month to gut a PCP of all its contents, sort, and tag components for processing. He went on vacation for a week once, and I had one finished when he returned. He went to my supervisor and stated, "Get him out of here." I got moved to cleaner work in assembly/upgrade of PCPs.

I didn't even pick up a soldering iron for the first few months until I had moved over to the assembly section. Cleaner work, but still not fun. The best part of this job was my ability to assemble the Automatic Data Process (ADP) drawers by climbing into the cabinet, where no-one else in the section could fit.

It earned me the nickname "shim stock" (a skinny laminated material for making shims used as spacers when assembling items). You would peel the layers back until the shim was the correct thickness. I had a 29" inch waist at the time, now I am up to 42 inches.

Of course, my co-op program would end with my high school graduation, but historically "Vo-techers" would be re-hired full time after graduation but it was not guaranteed. If there were no vacant positions to be hired into, the process would stop there. At this time however, the depot was involved in the maintenance of nearly everything the Army owned, missile equipment, tracked vehicles, and wheeled vehicles with over 5,000 workers.

In my case, I graduated high school on Friday and went to work on Monday, a seamless transition. I was placed into a temporary program that was not to exceed three years, which did worry me some. At one point, I explored a career in the Army Reserves by taking the military occupational skills test for electronics. The potential travel component of such a career move scared me at the time, so I didn't pursue that. I underestimated the commitment and sacrifice a military career requires, I guess.

During the depot's fortieth anniversary celebration, I learned that there were only five employees that had reached forty years of service. Of the tens of thousands of employees that came and went over that forty-year period, they stayed on. I was certainly impressed with that and contemplated that I could perhaps achieve forty years of service. I was age seventeen when I started, I would only be 57 when I finished...hmmm.

Then, one day I was called into the office by the Division Chief. He wanted to know if I had any digital circuitry at Vo-Tech. I stated I had. He stated that the Nike-Hercules workload was leaving Letterkenny and that his Wage Grade 13 technicians needed retrained on HAWK. Raytheon would only do a class for ten students and there were only 8 technicians needing training. I was asked if I wanted to receive the training, and I accepted. Now I don't know if anyone reading this understands the importance that the US Army stresses about seniority and time-in-grade preference, but here I am a low grade "newbie" being asked to attend advanced system level training. Yes please!!

So, there I am sitting in a room a few weeks later in Building #370 with a room full of high-grade employees excelling at the training they were all struggling to complete. I quickly earned their respect, and we all passed the course. I went back to assembling Platoon Command Posts and later Continuous Wave Acquisition Radars (CWAR)s.

Meanwhile, at home I was attempting to raise and expand my family and mobile home on a single income, so when I was offered a permanent job in the Chassis Reconditioning Section on second shift, I accepted. The thought of being "temporary" scared me. There were many negative effects of being on night shift on family life, but there were some positives as well. Just a normal personal decision at work here.

Eventually my mother's leaking ulcers in her legs would require her to be confined to a nursing home, also known as "Piney Mountain Home", a long-term care facility affiliated with the United Brethren church denomination. Crystal and I would agree to purchase the house that I grew up in for 75% of its value ($21K of $28K) in exchange for allowing Dad to live with us. Since half of the real estate was Mom's, $14K would have needed to be borrowed or the real estate sold before PA state medical assistance would kick in and pay the daily rate. Today there is an act of the Pennsylvania government in effect that protects a certain amount of real estate assets for the other spouse.

The second shift job allowed me to shuttle my mother around to doctor visits, shopping, and other things during the day. It also allowed me to continuously fix and upgrade the house. After all, very little had been done about it in forty-plus years. It also had to be decluttered of all of the hoarding before we could even move into it.

One afternoon I was called into my Chassis Reconditioning supervisor's office and was informed that I needed to sign a paper that "I understand that this promotion was temporary, and I would revert back to my old pay grade without re-promotion rights." I asked, what promotion? He stated you are starting Monday in the System Test section as a Wage Grade 12 temporary promotion. Personnel records show you are "system trained" and there is a staffing shortage in the "front garage" (the area where all final system testing and repair is done).

Turns out, there was a travel related scandal in El Paso TX that happened over many years, involving many of the Wage Grade 12s and 13s. This resulted in an urgent need for anyone with the potential to keep the HAWK program on track.

Now I realize what just transpired over a course of many years, the unsolicited training I received resulted in an unsolicited promotion and now an increased level of **access**!

I completed this promotion period and returned to the Chassis Reconditioning section as a Wage Grade 5. I made a lot of mistakes in the System Test section, which is to be expected when one with very little experience is being promoted, but I gained a lot of knowledge from my **access** to the HAWK missile system and my co-worker mentors.

I continued to submit requests for promotion to Wage Grade 8 as next step normal progression through the Chassis Recondition section, but now I could, and did, submit applications for Wage Grade 10, 11, and 12 because now I am on record as holding a Wage Grade 12 position. Always mostly received "best qualified - not selected" but did eventually get promoted to Wage Grade 8. The point here is, without the Wage Grade 12 experience I would have been "not qualified" for anything above a Wage Grade 8. Somewhere a door is still open...

Chapter 6

Career

1991-2002

One afternoon, I am working at my bench in 1991 rebuilding a "High Voltage Regulator" for HAWK Improved High Powered Illuminator Radar (IHPIR), when this old guy I have never met before pulled a chair next to my bench and asked me some questions, 1. Are you willing to work second shift, 2. Are you willing to sign out these special tools (he had a list), and 3. Are you willing to travel? I stated yes to all three questions. He said "good, you are starting the next pay period as a Wage Grade 12 working for me in the front garage". Turns out, that was an unsolicited job interview!

I would later learn my new supervisor was a little bit different. He called cable assemblies "hoses" and wires "strings" and loved to hoard spare parts. He assigned me to testing noisy, greasy, and oily M192 Launchers but now I had greater **access** to the HAWK system. I gained a thorough knowledge of it.

For the HAWK program, I was able to travel to Huntsville, Alabama for system level training. It was here I was able to spend time with my uncle Clair and his family. Clair was the only one of my dad's family that moved out of Pennsylvania, so it was very rare to even see him and his family. Here I was able to visit them every week for several weeks and was even able to travel back to Pennsylvania with him one weekend. I can chalk my visit to Cracker Barrel on that road trip.

I was also able to travel to North Carolina, South Carolina, Massachusetts, Texas, New Mexico, Florida, and Amman, Jordan for HAWK new equipment fielding and training events. I was able to train the Israeli Air Force on the Phase III upgrade. I could have traveled to Israel, but I didn't.

The North Carolina trip was close enough to home, I could rent a car and come home to visit. I did that once as I remember after a blizzard came through Pennsylvania.

On a trip to New Mexico, I was able to take the whole family at the time over the road and rent an apartment for a month. It took about three or four days each way to drive. Ashley learned to swim on that trip.

On a trip to Florida, I was able to also rent an apartment, this time along the beach. Crystal drove the eighteen-hour trip with all three kids to Florida which was hard, but we were able to travel to Disney World, Universal Studios, Busch Gardens, and Gatorland. Ashley doesn't remember that trip, I guess she was too young. Don't spend a lot of your own money traveling with children under 5, wait until they are older.

On the trip to Jordan, I visited Jerash, Bethany Beyond the Jordan, the Dead Sea, Petra, and Mount Nebo.

I believe my traveling was difficult on my wife, she had to be the "single mother" back home while I was gone. She eventually quit her full-time job at the Navy Support Activity as her schedule filled beyond capacity with the birth of our third child Ashley. Eventually HAWK would be phased out by the Army and National Guard and be replaced by the PATRIOT Air Defense System. So now, I had **access** to that system too.

I am intentionally spelling this as all capital letters, because originally the original equipment manufacturer would unofficially break the system name out as an acronym. "Phased Array TRacking Intercept Of Target". On the PATRIOT program, I traveled to North Carolina, Texas, New Mexico, Washington, Germany, Kuwait, Saudi Arabia, and Korea while working for Letterkenny.

On the trip to attend training in El Paso, TX I was able to rent an apartment instead of a hotel. The apartment per month was cheaper than a hotel room. This allowed me to host Crystal, Anthony, and Daryl for a week. Crystal had to lead the family on this airplane trip, having never traveled it before. Ashley wasn't born yet. We traveled all around El Paso to White Sands missile range, Alamogordo, and Carlsbad caverns.

Today, resource managers in the government frown upon the use of apartments for official travel duty. Makes you wonder if they are truly dedicated to saving money, or just taking away personal freedom…

Much later, on a trip to Germany, I was able to take Crystal and Ashley along. I took a day off work to visit Paris, France. Crystal always wanted to go to France, but I would not recommend attempting to commute to and visit France all in one day.

On a trip to Massachusetts, we were able to pull Ashley from school and visit Boston as an educational trip.

Ultimately, the PATRIOT Radar Set would become that electronic system of systems that I would fully understand and would excel in. Nothing before or after would ever come close. I still had the steep learning curve at first, but it never really plateaued like everything else I got involved in. I was always learning and getting better.

When the PATRIOT overhaul program first started at Letterkenny, it was a very intermittent and underfunded program. There were as many as sixty fire units of equipment bought and fielded to the Army. At that rate, the nearly 100 radars the US Army owned would take forty-plus years to overhaul through a continuous cycle.

The program started with Production Set 1 because it was the oldest. A production set was a Radar and Engagement Control Station. It used to take them eighteen weeks/seven days to test a radar, and the depot would only be able to complete one or two radars per year at that rate.

The overhaul program was always over budget and behind schedule. The former NIKE-Hercules team members that were assigned to make it work really did not know what they were doing.

The Production Set 1 process was so bad, they could not sell it off to the battalion commander at Ft. Polk, Louisiana. He would not sign for it, just too unreliable.

Eventually, Mr. Bryant at the Aviation and Missile Command (AMCOM) would develop a process for determining which radars were in the worst shape by a process called Technical Inspection (TI). Then the Production Sets started to be overhauled out of order.

Persian Gulf War-1 was started to liberate Kuwait from Iraqi control. After that, the PATRIOT system earned an improved reputation as the Army's superior air defense weapon. It received a lot of exposure on television during that war.

The travel requirements for PATRIOT would then become intense. The system received increases in funding that continued almost indefinitely. Quick Response Program, Mini Sweep-down Programs, and even major upgrades in hardware and software known as Configurations II and III. Once the global fleet was modified by one PATRIOT project, we would be going back again and again with the follow-on modifications.

But even with increased funding, there were still limitations at Letterkenny to get them overhauled and working again. I found a sense of purpose now, increasing production throughput by reducing test time. I became a highly motivated system test mechanic.

Instead of arguing with my "senior" co-workers about what an appropriate fix should be (they certainly did enough of that), I would just wait for them to break, and fix the system before they go back.

Often, they would be dumb enough to ask, "What did you do to it?"

I would usually respond, "I did what I tried to tell you to do."

Of course, some would become impressed (and others disgusted).

I eventually became perhaps the smartest and fastest Radar system test mechanic at the depot at that time, teaching others to excel with me. I don't mean I was the smartest person by any means, only the smartest on how the radar operated. I didn't care about sports or reading books, all of my available brain cells went into understanding how the radar worked, and the remainder of the system controlled it. God had gifted me with that attribute.

Engineers at Raytheon would eventually become impressed (and sometimes disgusted) with my comprehensive knowledge of the system as our paths crossed performing modification and fielding events for PATRIOT. I fixed several radars while they were still conferring with their "subject matter experts" at Pelham NH and Andover, MA on a diagnosis and repair plan.

I was often one of only two depot workers at work on a Saturday, because I was trusted to get things done, and got them done. I earned that trust, but God gifted me with ethics and intelligence.

Coworkers played 500 Rummy and Uno with playing cards or Solitaire on a computer, while I worked. An example of the mentorship they provided me with was, "We are waiting on the radar to warm up because a radar never works right for the first hour or so." I even bought into their theory for a while until my first radar fielding.

On my first radar fielding of a Radar Set at Fort Bliss, we got the radar all warmed up and working and declared to the accepting Battery Maintenance Warrant Officer that we were ready to sell, i.e., perform System Integration and Check-Out (SICO). He declared that he was not going to accept it today, he would accept it tomorrow morning from a cold start.

Apparently, the battlefield requirement for PATRIOT required that the system be ready to fire twenty minutes from arriving at the tactical site. This was in complete inverse of how I was "trained" at the depot. While a crock of crap they fed me. I would not have known that without **access** to the SICO process.

At that point forward, when testing radars, I would turn the system on and start baseline testing immediately at the start of my shift. It took more than twenty minutes for digital diagnostics to run so the analog hardware should be ready for analog testing. If a failure occurs at cold temps, I would be out there, diagnosing it when the air was cold. If the radar only failed when it was hot, then there would be some "sweat equity" involved. That was my job after all.

I would often be assisted by before Sid, the original "Vo-techer" that I talked about in Chapter 4, he was now an engineer at the depot. He would assist when we would get "stumped" by some unusual performance test results on the performance test pattern range. I learned more about the operation of phased arrays from him than anyone, when we experienced a catastrophically failing antenna performance test on the pattern range. The experience contradicted a lot of the theory training we had received from Raytheon trainers. They just didn't know because they didn't have the **access** I had.

Under my leadership testing was reduced to eight to twelve weeks/six days. My division chief at the time Tom McMath bet me a steak dinner once, that testing Radar Set through baseline, parametric, and performance tests could not be done in twelve weeks. He paid up at Greenvillage Diner at lunchtime after three radars in a row were completed in the eight to twelve-week timeframe! I guess somehow, I understood there was an urgent need to improve.

What I didn't know at the time was that there was a PATRIOT project being developed in AMCOM that was driving the requirement to improve repair turnaround time on the radar, and ultimately increase the workload through the depot. It was called the Recapitalization program (a.k.a. Recap), a program led by Mr. Yurko to ensure that no radar would be in the field for more than ten years. Turns out, there was someone else in the world who understood there was an urgent need to improve the process. I would later work for him in Chapter 10 of this memoir.

That twelve-week test schedule eventually became the requirement for the PATRIOT Recapitalization program, which is funded by the US Army as a one battalion per year maintenance program. So, under my leadership (working in a non-leadership position) I established a production flow for a program that has been successful for almost 20 years now. You won't read about that in the KennyLetter (The local depot newsletter publication)!

I am not saying I was perfect. If I had to pay for everything that I hooked up wrong or plugged in wrong, I would have worked many years for free.

Chapter 7

The Earth Shakes

2003-2004

At some point the AMCOM decided that its GS12 and 13 Readiness Directorate "Logistics Agency Representatives (LAR)s" needed training to help them better support the Air Defense Battalions that they are tasked to support under Army Regulation 700-4. Their leader Alan Kessler developed a plan to send them to Letterkenny to receive training.

As I trained them and we interacted, they concluded that my technical ability could be useful in the Logistics Assistance Program career field. I was asked if I would be interested in becoming a "mission essential" LAR working with them. It would be a General Schedule Grade 12 position, so there would be an immediate pay increase, and promotion potential.

This would mean permanent change of station and physical condition requirements at play. Such a drastic career move scared me at the time, so I didn't pursue it. I was also starting to get involved in the Mongul Church worship team and acoustic String Band as a violin player at the time and was involved with the Lurgan Township Lions Club.

Sometime later, it was determined by the Aviation and AMCOM, the agency that funded and commanded Letterkenny at the time) that Turkey would be purchasing excess HAWK equipment from the United States, and that the depot would be rebuilding it and fielding it in Turkey. As one of the only remaining depot employees that knew HAWK, I was pulled off PATRIOT to test and repair HAWK Launchers destined for Turkey.

I was devastated by this event; one I perceived as a giant step backwards in my career. I no longer had any interest in HAWK, and I never lost anything in the country of Turkey I needed to get or see. So, I revisited the AMCOM LAR job opportunity. We discussed it as a family at a table at the Shippensburg Pizza Hut, and I was approved to **access** this next career phase.

I started applying for them on USAJOBs, but did not get selected right away, but eventually I was selected.

I will always remember my last travel duty for Letterkenny. I was to "sell off" Production Set 77 Radar to Battalion 6-52 in Germany. The same Mr. Bryant I talked about in Chapter 6 was there to oversee the process. He thought he understood the process (based on his history of other Letterkenny products) and instructed us to bring the radar inside the garage to get it ready for SICO as that would take a while. Then ready, we would take it outside to radiate and demonstrate to the Battalion

I told him it was already adjusted for this weather (25 degrees F), so we are ready to go outside now. It was obvious he didn't believe it; he hadn't even contacted the Battalion to come there yet.

By afternoon on Day 1, we had clean baseline test results. It took two days to get the Battalion there. We sold it off that same day. Mr. Bryant couldn't believe the improvement in quality.

They attempted to keep me at Letterkenny by promoting me to Wage Leader grade 13, but that didn't work. I was already mentally "departed from Letterkenny".

Chapter 8

Life in a New State

2004-2006

Now here is where this story gets really controversial. Is it divine **access** to take a world-wide deployable career position like AMCOM LAR, when you are directed to put God first, family second, and career only when it supports God and family?

After all, my oldest child is already deployable as a Marine, my middle child is recovering from a devastating motorcycle accident, and my youngest child was just as scared as I was by the thought of moving away from a stable home and school environment.

Was I simply devastated by a career event and being selfish? Was God opening the country of Turkey as my destiny or the AMCOM LAR career path for His purpose? I will never know for sure.

I will however always remember seeing my daughter crying in the back seat of our 1994 Ford Taurus Station Wagon from my packed-up 2002 Pontiac Grand Prix headed for Huntsville, AL in Oct. 2004. I will never forget that.

It just proves I am not perfect. For that I am truly sorry!

I arrived at Redstone Arsenal, Huntsville, AL to process at AMCOM and took the required three weeks of training. During that time, I was able to spend more time with Uncle Clair.

My job title was Equipment Specialist with the Readiness Directorate (a.k.a. AMCOM LAR) and would be providing logistics assistance to Army commands (ACOMs), Army service component commands (ASCCs), direct reporting units (DRUs) and other Army forces through the Logistics Assistance Program in accordance with Army Regulation 700-4.

AMCOM recognized that PATRIOT is a complex weapon system that needed subject matter experts to assist warfighters to maintain an affordable and achievable state of readiness.

I would be required now to achieve certification as an Acquisition Workforce Professional in Logistics Level II, as required recently by an act of congress. This means I would have **access** to new training, because you have to be in a certain position to **access** the training modules.

My first duty station would be Fort Bliss, in El Paso TX. I checked into an apartment on a six-month lease alone, with only what would fit into my Grand Prix. Since I accepted a position without Permanent Change of Station (PCS) moving expenses authorized, I would have no bed or other furniture other than a Lane cedar chest that fit in the back seat. My thought process was that since I was a "newbie" at this job, I would not be here long. I would soon be deployed to Southwest Asia.

I would be assigned to support the 3rd Battalion, 2nd Air Defense Artillery (ADA) brigade (a.k.a. Battalion 3-2) located there. Now I had **access** to all of the PATRIOT motor pool training sites.

Since I had never been in the military assigned to an ADA battalion, I had to learn a lot about military command structure, weapon certification tables, and readiness reporting procedures very quickly. After all, I was now mission essential and could be deployed with my brigade at any time.

Of course, I excelled at technical assistance due to my knowledge of the system, especially the radar. After all, depot level (-50) is the highest level of maintenance in accordance with AR 700-10. All of my co-workers were only at Intermediate (-34) level, having only been exposed to the depot for a short time.

I was told very early in this LAP process that my value to the Warfighter would be determined on their first request for assistance. If I could not provide them a relevant solution when asked, they would probably not call me again.

The ADA Brigades at Fort Bliss would do simulated deployments to the field to test their ability to meet weapon system gunnery table training requirements. My first field visit was to a Firing Battery in a white SUV (I remember scratching the heck out of it getting there through the desert vegetation) during a training exercise at McGregor Range Camp, NM. My visit resulted in me diagnosing their Beam Steering Processor fault immediately with no parts required.

I eventually did get deployed to Camp As-Sayliyah, Qatar for 120 days, so I vacated the apartment in El Paso. I drove to Pennsylvania and flew to Qatar from there so I could see the family again.

Now that I am being deployed, someday it will be time to move the family to El Paso with me back to my permanent duty station. Just not sure how to pay for that.

I really didn't know what to expect from a deployment. I know it would not be as intense or austere as the deployments my son Anthony experienced as a CH-53E mechanic in the US Marine Corp, but after all PATRIOT did support the march to Baghdad, Iraq during Operation Iraqi Freedom. Many other AMCOM LARs had to support that effort.

A maintenance unit service member even got held hostage once. Remember Jessica Lynch? She was in the 507th maintenance company that supported PATRIOT, part of 11th ADA Brigade

I arrived in Qatar and was picked up at the airport by the LAR I was replacing. We arrived at a housing neighborhood, and I was informed that I would be sharing a two-story house with one other person and driving an SUV to the camp each day…sweet!

I arrived at work the next day and learned that Camp As-Sayliyah was the place where troops went for rest and relaxation from Iraq and Afghanistan. The Brigade that I was going to be supporting was not a tactical unit, but an Army Field Support Battalion with equipment in an Army Prepositioned Stock storage. A desirable and safe location, with few technical challenges. If that would not be considered a gravy deployment by a reasonable person, I am not sure what is.

I would eventually complete my deployment and return to PA to pack up the family and move them to El Paso, TX. Nothing was prepared prior to my arrival, but we packed up the 28' ABF moving trailer I rented with much of our stuff. We left a lot of stuff behind because Daryl would need a place to live. He was not coming with us.

Crystal, Ashley, and I drove to El Paso, on a route through Moore OK to visit Cynthia, a cousin of Crystal's. We spent an extra day or so there, and then moved on. Once we arrived in town, Ashley was impressed by the elaborate bridge designs along I-10. We would later learn that we had to pay an annual bridge tax as El Paso County vehicle owners.

We arrived in El Paso and stayed at the Residence Inn until we could get into the house we rented on Lakewood Ave. We settled on Vista Ysleta UMC as our new church home, one of my new coworkers Tom attended there. I became active on the worship team, Crystal became active on the video presentation team, and Ashley became active in the youth group. Pretty much the same church involvement as we all had at Mongul church.

Ashley would enroll at Eastwood High School and complete ninth grade there. I am sure that it was a challenge for her there with everyone else in the classes being bi-lingual.

Crystal found El Paso to be a challenge as well, with all of the traffic and limited job opportunities. Every job required fluent bilingual ability, which none of us had. I think if she were elected to a position of power, she would transfer all of El Paso County back to Mexico with an apology "sorry we took this from you in the 19th century, you can have it back now".

Eventually, the AMCOM LAR job would turn into a proposed two-year PCS to Osan Air Base, South Korea to support 35th ADA Brigade. There is an Army Material Command regulation (AMC-R 700-23) that covers PCS orders and its allowable exceptions. None of the exceptions applied to my situation.

I found a clause in the AMC regulation that mentioned "transfers to a non-mission essential position" interesting. I started submitting applications for everything in the GS-12 pay grade on the "USAJOBs" website. That clause would not get me out of this PCS, but I would at least be able to "plant some seeds".

The family made it clear that they were not interested in traveling overseas, so it was decided that I would go alone as a one-year tour, and they would return to PA. After all, we still had a partially furnished house there.

I had a co-worker ask me one day if he could take my place in Korea. I told him that I strongly supported the Make-A-Wish foundation, so if he "wished" to take my place I would strongly support that! We submitted our proposal to AMCOM, and it was denied. It seems God was providing me **access** to South Korea, so I won't be truly alone. God will be with me.

I arranged to put everything in storage in El Paso at government expense, put Ashley on a plane back to PA in time for the "Creation Fest" festival, and Crystal would drive back to PA alone in the Taurus wagon. I know that was hard for her, but when she is determined enough (and God is with her), there is nothing she can't accomplish.

Chapter 9

Life in a Foreign Country

2006-2007

In July 2006, I landed at Incheon Airport, and was escorted by the Senior Command Representative for Korea, Bob, and was set up in a fancy hotel in Seoul for in-processing at Yongsan Garrison. Later, I would learn later he was allegedly running a scam to stay long term in a hotel instead of getting permanent housing, and setting up all new LARs at the hotel was part of his scam to get business for them. I was later interviewed by investigators on that case.

I would be replacing co-worker Tony, who had a second-floor apartment he was leasing from a local resident in Pyeongtaek, just outside the Osan AB fence. It was expected that I would take over the same apartment and crappy car, so I did. $25,000 per year, all paid in cash in a lump-sum, which I was reimbursed for by the US government. I was later interviewed by investigators during a security-clearance renewal on why such a large amount of cash left my checking account, go figure.

I signed out all of my appliances from the air base housing department, and they were delivered by a Korea moving company. I was impressed, the Korean guy balanced the washing machine on his back and carried it up the steps and in the door. He made it look easier than the traditional two-person lift.

I would be assigned to Battalion 1-43 ADA split between Suwon AB, and Osan AB, with full **access** to both. I would be assigned a nine-passenger van as my government transportation, and a cell phone as I was on call 24/7.

Now I have full **access** to the PATRIOT tactical operations!

My office would be at Suwon AB, so I was now commuting from Osan to Suwon daily, through "crazy" traffic. People here in the US think that "crazy" traffic is rush hour in Harrisburg PA. I call "crazy" traffic, people constantly blowing through stop signs, busses cutting off other traffic by pulling over the crosswalk into the middle of an intersection to be the first to go when the light turns green, and motor-scooters with nine propane bottles strapped on the back of it weaving in and out of traffic.

There were some positive things that came from this experience. I got to tour Seoul on my own, went on a bus trips skiing and to Yoido Full Gospel Church to include Prayer Mountain. I went on a US Air Force sponsored bus trip to the Demilitarized Zone with **access** to the building where the armistice was signed. I was actually standing in the North Korea at one point since the meeting building and desk are actually sitting on the line. I became involved in the worship team with my violin, the group was named "Solid ROK" band.

The chapel system at Osan AB has multiple campuses and services to support the quantity and faith differences of the thousands of airmen and family stationed in the region. The contemporary service was in the evening at the main chapel building.

I was invited to attend the local "Hospitality House" by members of the chapel. This is a mission sponsored by Cadence International in Songtan. Songtan is a little town riddled with sex trafficking and drinking establishments, so it was refreshing to find others worshiping God in such a hellhole. I was there almost every weekend.

I was able to fix a Radar Set on Osan Air Base that no one had not been able to diagnose and fix in over two years, as described by the battalion maintenance warrant officers stationed there with responsibility for it.

While I was there, a Letterkenny team showed up to install a Mini-sweep modification on my battalion. Now a team that I would normally be on as a Wage Grade 12, I was assisting as a GS-12. That was cool. I did whatever I could to support them. One day, they needed compressed gas at Osan AB to run their cutting torches. I met the local delivery truck, loaded the big gas bottle down the center of the van, and drove through the gate at Osan AB with my arm resting on it. I probably would not try that again today.

I received an "Achievement Medal for Civilian Service" for work logistical support of the M-860 trailer. My battery warrant officer came into my office and informed me that he had a Launching Station had broken down along the highway with a bad brake chamber. The new in box unit had two ports and one removed from the trailer had three ports.

I was able to get the procedure for making this work through my **access** to the depot and was able to trade two port chambers with three port chambers at the local Army Prepositioned Stock maintenance facility by providing the Letterkenny provided procedure to them. My Army Material Command boss with over thirty years' service had never seen such cross-command cooperation like this happen before, especially so quickly.

Eventually I would be offered a non-mobile position back in Huntsville, AL, working for the Lower Tier Project Office (LTPO), working for Mr. Yurko whom I mentioned earlier in Chapter 6. This was a growth from a seed I planted back in Chapter 7.

My Senior Command Representative (SCR) in Korea, Bob, worked tirelessly to stop the transfer from Korea, but I reminded him of that AMC-R 700-23 regulation that sent me there. He was so pissed off; he took the issue all the way to the AMCOM Chief of Staff. He failed to stop it. I received my PCS order, so I started packing and shipping my stuff.

He was successful in delaying it for two months by direction of the local Army Field Support Brigade Commander. All that did was provide me with more time to find a house in Alabama for the family. Crystal and Ashley drove down and signed a lease on a house on Brass Oak Drive, Madison, AL.

I am about to get **access** to the entire PATRIOT project command structure!

Chapter 10

Life in Another New State

2007-2010

In March 2007, I flew back to El Paso to get my Grand Prix out of storage and arrange for shipping my household goods to Madison AL. The car did not do so well in storage, the battery would not hold a charge very long. I had the battery tested at an AutoZone on Dyer Street, but then made a dumb decision not to change the battery there. I drove straight through to Alabama, never turning the car off other than for gas. I stopped to sleep at one point in Louisiana and left the car running. The battery was too hot to touch when I arrived in Alabama.

I stayed with my uncle Clair for a week but moved into the house in Madison after getting rear ended on Jordan Lane one day on the way to work. My household goods would not arrive for another week, so I bought a reclining lawn chair, a washer/dryer, refrigerator, and an LCD television. I slept on the lawn chair.

Crystal and Ashley came down in June after she completed tenth grade at Chambersburg Area Senior High School, and we settled in. She attended Bob-Jones High School, the house we leased was picked due its proximity to this school with great reviews on the internet.

We settled on a church family known as Cross-Pointe church. Not a large church, but a rapidly growing church. They had two services, both identical in content. We chose to go to the second service. They used a name tag process so people would be able to greet or address you. Ashley quickly adapted to the youth group.

Although my new duty station was Redstone Arsenal, my job would be located off the arsenal on Wynn Drive at a facility leased by the government. I did absolutely nothing for the first several months. They told me I would be in charge of Sweep-down 7 modification projects, but the modification kits were still in the procurement/production phase. Why was I brought here? It was God's plan.

I would be required now to continue to achieve certification as an Acquisition Workforce Professional in Logistics Level III, so I would have an increased level of **access** to training.

Eventually, my wife would find full time employment with the Army Corps of Engineers. I believe she enjoyed her job there.

A co-worker announced his retirement under a reduction in force early separation authority, and I would be assigned his duties. I would be in charge of the Integrated Diagnostic Support System project, not Sweep-down 7. I had two contracts that supported me, about four contractors at CAS Inc, and three contractors at Raytheon. I would submit a budget request for $2M and would be given about $1.4M. That is the strategy I was taught by Mr. Yurko, request more than you need so when you are cut you still have what you need. I would submit funding requests to withdraw this money to procure computers, software, and accessories to perform maintenance on PATRIOT radars, my area of expertise. We also did fiber optic cable repair.

I would provide funding to the PATRIOT Field Office to procure these materials, so I would have to occasionally travel to Chambersburg. I would now be able to visit Daryl and look in on the house. These trips often became work trips at night to repair something there. I was even promoted to GS-13, after my boss achieved the authority to reengineer the early separated position.

We would travel often on short term trips to provide these items and training directly to the battalion and brigade maintenance personnel. At a fielding event at 6-52 ADA Germany, I took Crystal and Ashley along. We all took one day to tour Paris, France, Crystal has always wanted to go to Paris. The travel is more frequent, but for a much shorter duration.

I was also able to travel to Oklahoma, North Carolina, Texas, Kuwait, Bahrain, Qatar, and the United Arab Emirates for PATRIOT new equipment fielding and training events. I could have traveled to Greece, but I didn't. I just sent my contractors on that one.

I once had to brief the AMCOM Commander in his classified readiness briefing in the basement of building 5000 on the arsenal pertaining to a particular maintenance issue that I was very familiar with. That was exciting!

It was here in the project office that I would learn just how rare and special the PATRIOT sustainment program really was. As I stated before, Mr. Bryant was running the program based on the funding given to him.

Mr. Yurko took a completely different approach. He would run the program by giving the Pentagon a decision to make. Is PATRIOT your weapon of choice for air defense or not? If the answer is yes, then you need to fund it at a level that keeps the system recapitalized every ten years.

He briefed them that if they funded his program sufficiently to recapitalize one of ten battalions per year, then no battalion would ever be older than ten years.

So, they funded his "little program" in fiscal year 1999 as a pilot program, and it worked! Readiness increased and sustainment cost decreased. PATRIOT recapitalization is now in iteration two and still running.

No one person has ever generated the magnitude of funding and employment opportunity at Letterkenny Army Depot than he had/has. He is gone now, a victim of his constant smoking habit.

I was proud now to be a part of the program at the front end (project), not just at the back end (workload).

But then my scope of work and life would change again. There were forces at work that would put me on track to have me spend more time in foreign countries than at home.

The Koreans decided to buy a used PATRIOT system from Germany and signed a Foreign Military Sales (FMS) case for logistical support. The United Arab Emirates (UAE) decided to buy new PATRIOT systems from Raytheon and signed an FMS case to procure and field them. The Taiwanese decided to buy more PATRIOT from Raytheon, now that production has restarted. They signed an FMS case as well.

The Korean FMS case sent me there once to Camp Henry for what was supposed to be ninety days. I was able to turn it in sixty-five days through a strategy that worked out for me. I refused to brief anyone else on the IDSS fielding events, then an emergent requirement came up.

I was proud to be a subject matter expert representing the US in Korea, but the language barriers were tough to overcome. The Raytheon provided training to Koreans always resulted in some request for clarification or amplification.

It was UAE that was going to affect me the most. I was informed I would be assigned as the SICO team lead, responsible to "transfer" the new equipment from the US ownership to UAE ownership. For nine fire units, this would take over a year on site in the UAE.

The Emirates (as the people were known there), were much smarter than the Koreans on PATRIOT, they had done their research by talking to their neighbors Saudi Arabia and Kuwait. They knew what to buy from Raytheon, and when they were potentially being taken advantage of. The leaders possessed a very high English comprehension level.

But the potential travel requirements were just too overwhelming. I told a co-worker once, "If I wake up in the morning, and my only choices that day are Korea, Taiwan or UAE, then I will be gone." Now, if I had mentally taken ownership of this concept, I would have profited a lot in excess meals per diem, and would literally have a million IHG points, but I was not interested. I was a US citizen with two houses here and planned to spend my life in those houses.

So, I started a negotiation with the chief of my old division at Letterkenny to return as an employee there. In the end, Wayne offered me two positions for both my wife and I. God is still at work providing **access**!

The kicker was that I would have to accept a downgrade from GS-13 to GS-12. I accepted that.

In the meantime, since PATRIOT would need to be totally redesigned around parts available on the market today, I had **access** to all of the critical design reviews and pre-production reviews with the contractor. I also had a five-year VISA to visit the country of UAE, which is very rare for a US citizen.

But here we go again! Was I simply devastated by another career event and being selfish? Was God opening a return to Letterkenny as my destiny, or was traveling to new foreign countries his purpose? I will never know for sure.

There was surely the risk of hurting my daughter again by leaving her behind, this time on her own. I guess I justified it by thinking, she was of college age now, it is reasonable and customary to leave children on their own at this point in their life. I remember crying when I broke the frame on her Van-Gogh painting during the packing and moving of stuff out of the Alabama house. The stress of negatively affecting her again was overwhelming.

Crystal and I also continued to pay the expenses on the house in Alabama and continued to visit her. These trips often became work trips to repair something at the house.

Chapter 11

Return to the Homestead

2010 – 2020

In Dec. 2010, we were back at the homestead. We arrived to find Daryl had done nothing to prepare for our arrival. Lots to move, clean, refurbish, unpack, and maintain. We also learned that we were going to need more room in the house. We tore down the old two car garage my dad built fifty years ago and contracted with Woody to add a new two car attached garage with rooms above, and expansion of a bedroom, and addition of a closet.

My new job would be the PATRIOT Logistics Management Specialist (LMS), as Fred had already announced his retirement, the reason I was able to return. I would be a Contracting Officer's Representative (COR) for the repair and return contract with Raytheon, initiating all delivery orders, coordinating carcass shipment, tracking delivery receipt of the repaired material, and authorizing payment to the contractor.

I also would advise and assist the shop floor personnel performing the recapitalization effort, and work to ensure they had the technical data they needed.

In 2012, my division chief Wayne would announce he was retiring early. My thought process was, now I could potentially get promoted back to a GS-13 again. I applied for it, was interviewed, and I accepted it. Later I would learn that I was the only applicant that answered the question "which comes first in priority, quality or schedule?" In my answer, I gave three examples of where qualified defects negatively affected both cost and schedule both.

I would be required now to achieve certification as an Acquisition Workforce Professional in Production and Quality Management (PQM) Level II. This training really changed a lot of my thought processes, the intent of the course was to streamline processes. I continue to this day, thinking about reducing steps and streamlining processes everywhere I go, even fast-food restaurants.

One of the takeaways from this training for me was thinking about a workflow in reverse. The instructors used an analogy of floating down a river in a boat. Floating down the river, you get to see scenery along the way of course, but when you travel upstream you get an entirely different view. A view into every tributary that feeds the river.

That is what I am kind of doing in this book, looking backwards into the causes and the effects of my life. While I was living it, I wasn't able to see these as clearly.

Material Requirement Planning (MRP) was an important concept discussed there, but they were not obsessed with the concept like Letterkenny was. Letterkenny would excess items that hadn't been used in ninety days, and then order it back later.

I would learn in PQM class an acronym "TIMWOOD", representing seven forms of waste in a manufacturing (or remanufacturing) process; Time, Inventory, Movement, Waiting, Overproduction, Overprocessing and Defects. At Letterkenny, they invented an eighth form of waste, an obsession with inventory reduction. I started keeping track of the items excessed (I had **access** to the enterprise resource planning tool), and what was reordered again later because they were needed. I stopped counting at over $700K.

No sooner did I take the seat at my new desk as Division Chief in 2012, than management had chosen to make structural changes to my division, which is probably why Wayne retired early. I was not going to be able to replace my vacated LMS position, that function was being transferred to another directorate and they were taking the position with it.

Then sequestration hit in 2013. Sequestration was a result of the Legislative and Executive branches of the US government that were unable to do their jobs and agree on a budget to fully fund the government. The Army's budget would be frozen for years. I was not going to be able to replace anyone that retired or resigned from my division. Over time, I slowly watched my division staffing go from 237 persons to 196 persons.

So, what did I do? I decided to go to war with the Letterkenny Army Depot management! After all, I was the only person there (command or subordinate) to comprehensively understand the strategic national importance of the PATRIOT Air Defense system. The only one to have worked on the equipment as an Electronics Mechanic, supported the field as an AMCOM LAR, managed a project under direction of the Program Executive Office – Missiles and Space, and back! It was my duty to resist stupidity, or so I thought.

I started submitting requests for overtime on the prescribed Army Material Command forms. I was challenged by management, "these need to be substantiated by a higher echelon command." I called my old boss at LTPO, Mr. Yurko, who provided the necessary statement of need signed by the Program Executive Office Missile and Space - Lower Tier Program Manager, a Military Grade O6.

My former Deputy Director Larry thought the lower tier meant lower priority somehow. He was wrong! There are two tiers in the atmosphere for air defense purposes, upper and lower tier.

Now depot management was forced to approve the overtime requests. They, of course, made it as difficult as possible. I have my production assistant now engaged in nothing else but meeting the data requirements for the overtime request, but I won the overtime battle. My division was at that point in time the only division in the Army Material Command system of five "hard iron" depots working overtime during sequestration. The word got out to the other AMCOM depot working aviation (Corpus Christi, TX) of this fact, then they started working it too. How do I know this? I had **access** to the Industrial Base Review meeting agenda and minutes!

Management was pissed, but I was supporting my program.

I partially won the staffing battle as well during an AMCOM general officer visit. There was a change of command at AMCOM, and the Major General was coming to see his depots. As a Division Chief, I was required to be a tour guide in Bldg. 370. I was specifically told by my management not to use acronyms on the tour, as he would not be able to understand them.

When I arrived in the section Cooler Liquid Electron Tube (CLET) rebuild area I stopped, and stated the following to the group: "Sir, I am not supposed to use acronyms on this tour, but you are going to hear the acronym CLET during your readiness briefings in the basement of building 5000 every week (I was the only employee at LEAD to have ever been to those meeting during my time at Redstone), because the CLET is the highest failure rate item on the radar worldwide.

"This section is the only place in the world where these are recapitalized."

He responded "Yes, I have already heard this acronym, what is the problem?"

I proceeded to tell Major General the entire background of the CLET at the depot, factory, and field like no-one else there could. I accentuated the fact that although I have plenty of funding from AMCOM, I do not have the staffing authorization here to complete the work to match the failure rate per month.

He directed my commander (his subordinate) to release and approve my open recruit fill requests. Now management is really pissed! I had disobeyed an order and jumped the chain of command. If I had not been a civilian employee, they would have used the Uniform Code of Military Justice against me for sure.

The Major General would later return for a follow-on tour, but I was exempted from it... go figure. I recognized that this may be time for another career change. It appears that I am winning battles with a score of 2-0 in my favor, but it is unlikely that I will win the war and be able to retire from this position in the year 2020 while acting this unprofessional. War is hell!

After twenty-seven months of that torture, I landed a lower grade position acting as a cone of protection from going insane. The best part of that job was working side by side with my daughter Ashley performing commodity management functions.

Next, I started applying for jobs at Navy Support Activity, Mechanicsburg. Perhaps I will be able to make it to retirement from there, the next closest installation to where I lived.

Chapter 12

Stress Reduction

2017-2020

In March 2017, I started as a Logistics Management GS-12 at NAVSUP Weapon System Support (WSS). I would be assigned as Program Manager on portions of the shipboard systems installed on Cruisers and Destroyers. It would be a pay decrease, as a different locality pay region.

I rode the Capital Area Transit bus from Shippensburg to Naval Support Activity to reduce miles on the cars, and out of pocket expenses for fuel. Why not, I figured, the Navy is paying for the bus tickets. I didn't like waiting for the bus in the afternoon, however, it made for a longer workday. I would get nothing done for weeks because I had no official training on anything in Navy databases, therefore I had to earn **access** to one database at a time. But there was knowledge to be obtained through that **access** as well.

I would be assigned as the program manager for the Common Display System. I learned, ironically, that display monitors installed on a ship are negatively affected by humidity and are not hermetically sealed as I would have concluded they would be... go figure. One ship had ten monitors fail over one ninety-six-hour holiday weekend.

I would later be assigned as Program Manager for the MK-41 Vertical Launching System, which in some ways is more impressive than a PATRIOT Launching Station. When a PATRIOT missile launch sequence is initiated, it simply punches through the canister front cover and blows out the rear cover of the canister, damaging the canister to the point that it must be overhauled. MK-41 must fire multiple missile types, repetitively, and not get damaged since it sits down in the hull of the ship. Cell hatch assemblies must open in time to allow the missile to fly, and vents must open to vent the exhaust gasses produced by their rocket motors.

I can now sit and watch a science fiction movie involving Destroyer DDG-53, identify the components of the ship and watch missiles fire from the MK-41 toward alien machines attacking it. If I would have still been limited to television as my only knowledge **access**, I would probably believe that DDG-53 was destroyed in that fight.

Army and Navy maintenance concepts are very different. The Navy does not have depots, they have contractors that perform depot level repairable items. Nothing gets done without a contract or delivery order that takes months to award, and then more months to repair.

The MK-41 was largely supported by a Performance Based Logistics (PBL) contract with Lockheed-Martin. A PBL contract is supposed to result in an outcome, requisitions filled. Turns out the contractor didn't really respect it as a PBL contract, they wanted to be paid for every repair just like on a repair and return requirements delivery order contract. There were backorders for MK-41 spares all of the time, and the contractor didn't care. Their effects on system readiness were called Navy Casualty Reports (CAS-REPs). This upset me greatly, because Raytheon took the PATRIOT PBL contract seriously and performed highly to ensure the fleet had stock on hand to fight and there were no Army Commander's Critical Items Report (CCIRs). Raytheon was financially penalized on their PBL contract for unfilled requisitions.

Things that took four hours to repair at Letterkenny, took months or years to repair through a contractor's facility. I had a MK-41 cell hatch assembly on contract with an 870-day repair turnaround time. After all, it is simply a 125-pound door assembly with an internal heater and hinges. We would recapitalize a 43,000-pound Radar Set in 400 days at Letterkenny.

I would eventually manage multiple Performance Based Logistics PBL contracts, and AN/SPY-1D Radar (similar to the Army's AN/TPY-2 radar), the Close in Weapon System, and the new AN/SPY-6 radar to be installed on future Destroyers. Part of that function was to report the status of the contract to Admirals and Senior Executive Service civilians.

While at WSS, I tried to get every contractor I was allowed to communicate with directly to understand Material Requirements Planning (MRP). Most would not even order their first part until they received a funded delivery order. I even offered Letterkenny Army Depot to Lockheed-Martin as a potential partnership opportunity to reduce turn-around on the MK-41 cell hatch. They apparently saw no value in it, they did nothing but have Letterkenny sign a non-disclosure agreement on the technical data.

I tried to get my co-workers to understand that MRP was the key to getting things down quickly, but they determined that legally there was nothing they could do differently in their process.

I tried to get the legal office to approve changes to contract statement of work templates to require MRP, and they vehemently opposed that concept. I would write in my final out-processing survey the following: "I call Building 410 (at Navy Support Activity), Station 410 now, because it has become more of an emergency management agency than a supply chain management agency." "The attorneys and inspectors general have a destructive level of influence over the contracting officers and program managers here that appears to be irreversible."

Eventually, I was commended by WSS management for my efforts to improve repair turnaround time and was even promoted back to GS-13 as an incentive to stay longer, but I retired in Nov. 2020 as soon as I had achieved my forty years of federal service. That was the goal I had started out with a long time ago.

I even retired from the government while on COVID-19 pandemic directed telework authorization. Who retires from telework, to stay home?

Now looking back as I write this today, I believe Letterkenny Army Depot has improved a lot from a chain of command perspective.

The commander is gone (normal part of the process), the deputy to the commander is gone (allegedly forced out), the chief of staff is gone (retired), the director of industrial operations is gone (went back to his old job), and the deputy director of industrial operations is gone (he was obviously loyal to the former deputy to the commander). Perhaps, I could have fought the battles longer. It certainly would have been lucrative financially.

The depot has lost a lot of talent along the way, however, and will never return to its former level of employee satisfaction and dedication to duty. I could start a family reunion now with all of the former Letterkenny employees that relocated to the Navy Support Activity.

Of course, that depends a lot on how you talk to them today. As I delivered FedEx Ground packages to them, they would say, "Just don't attempt to come back here to work, it's not as good as it was."

Crystal retired after having a mini-stroke in 2020, likely induced by stress at work. She was one of their highest performing workers as well, their loss again.

Sometimes, you just get tired of fighting.

Chapter 13

Semi - Retirement

2020 to present day

Next, I started delivering and picking up FedEx Ground packages in a cargo van for a contracted service provider in Chambersburg. Daryl had started working for them earlier, so I had some inside knowledge of what I was getting into.

I would get **access** to the distribution centers in Hagerstown and Newville. That was a learning experience as well. To see how items are handled (or mishandled) though processing was interesting.

The van had to traverse through mud holes and bouncing driveways as long as ¾ of a mile, which dropped and broke things as well.

Package pickup and delivery would be a part time job, delivering to what I called my "home route" a couple of days per week. I would get most of Lurgan and Letterkenny townships. I would deliver my packages directly to the kitchen counter.

In the Newville distribution center, Daryl and I were both loading and/or rearranging our packages in side-by-side bays on the same line.

Later, I started delivering to Letterkenny Army Depot and the surrounding business park area, so I was back to a full-time status. No-one liked delivering there, it was too difficult to gain **access** to the buildings and areas. I was accustomed to getting paid hourly to wait at locked gates and doors, so I excelled at that for about a year or so.

Eventually I would quit package delivery and pickup, it was for a combination of reasons.

1. It was just too physically demanding lifting packages up to 150 pounds alone every day. The team lift notes on the packages were ironic since I was a team of only one person. OSHA would have a field day with the safety violations involved in that job.
2. My route was twenty miles from one end to the other, so I had to break a lot of traffic laws to complete my work in a reasonable eight-hour period.
3. Cameras were installed to watch our every move. This is considered normal these days, but I had already worked forty years without that requirement.
4. I was embarrassed to deliver some of the packages after the mishandling that occurred. After all, a customer usually only sees the driver as the source of their damage.

In 2022, we sold the house in Alabama; it seems renting your house is not as profitable as one would assume. The real money was made by the rent significantly amortizing the mortgage over a 7.5-year period.

The delivery job helped pay the tax on the proceeds. In 2022, I made about $29K working, and paid about $19K in federal taxes.

We used some of the proceeds from the house sale to purchase a Class-C motorhome and put the remainder in savings. I call it our ten-year retirement plan to travel somewhere long distance each year. I bought a dolly to pull the Mini Cooper behind us.

I wasn't going to call the machine's purpose camping; I would call it traveling. I learned early I didn't like camping, although we do camp with Daryl's family a couple of times per year now.

We made one long distance trip to Pigeon Forge, Tennessee so far, but no others yet. We are still working and volunteering locally at the Lurgan Township Lions Club and Mongul Church (now known as Rising Hope United Brethren Church) and have grandchildren living close by, so it is not reasonable to travel often yet. At the time of this writing, I have seven grandchildren, Amelia, Derek, Wyatt, Olive, Blake, Miriam, and Aaron. I thank God they are all happy, healthy, and safe.

Now as I write this memoir, I am working as a school bus driver with **access** to school buildings and buses. It is my hope that I can earn some more "play money", as well as an unusual amount of time off. "Play money" is what I call funds over and above my annually adjusted retirement pay. Ironically, I will be working for one of my cousins. At least we will have a professional relationship, if not a personal one.

I am not sure what knowledge I will obtain from this new **access** as a Chambersburg School District contractor, but I shall take seriously the responsibility of handling the most precious packages of all... children.

I still have to deal with the cameras watching my every move. Something I will never get comfortable with. After all, none of us are perfect. Perfect workers would be both expensive and hard to deal with (since they are perfect in reference to the other members of the team).

Chapter 14

Conclusion

I am asking you now to consider the following, as you traverse through your cycle of life:

1. Are you simply going to rely on your own (or your friends/co-workers) knowledge and its associated power to get you through life?
2. Are you going to pray for the divine **access** to wisdom and guidance larger than yourself, potentially unlimited and everlasting knowledge?

I hope you choose number two, and I hope to see as many of you as possible by the river of life discussed in the Bible, the book of Revelation, Chapter 22.

It is a two-step process, there are no shortcuts.

1. I have to whatever it takes to gain **access** there to wait for you, AND
2. You have to do whatever it takes to gain **access** to me to find you there.